Surrendering to Love

in surrendering to love
i am losing who i was
in surrendering to love
i am becoming more me

Samuel L. Field

This is a work of personal expression,
it reflects the authors feelings and
may not reflect others perspective and intent

First published 2019 by YndFwd
www.yndfwd.com

Copyright © Samuel L. Field 2019
The moral rights of the author have been asserted.

All rights reserved. No part of this book may be reproduced or transmitted by any persons or entity, in any form or by any means, electronic or mechanical, including photocopying, recording, scanning, or by any information storage and retrieval system, without prior permission in writing from the publisher.

Cataloguing-in-Publication entry is available
from the National Library of Australia
http://catalogue.nla.gov.au

a gift
my life
love gave
i share it
it is love's
giving it back
yet i hold it still
stuck in partial surrender
i am slowly yielding to love
i gradually become love's
i truly become me

Contents

Where am i 7

Others and i 17

Love's purpose 33

Love gives hope 39

Trust love 51

Love is 61

Love is my hope 73

Worship 85

I am love's 103

often living by trust
only when i have to
not because i choose to
trusting in Love to hold on
rather than rise

Where Am I

What signs?

there are no sign posts to guide my way
they have been scrubbed clean
they're gone, removed, damaged, vacant
they're not there

i am off the path
but i am not forgotten
i am not where i wanted to be
but i am not alone

i cannot see the way
yet i know you're taking me home

Hope is a wayward bird

wayward bird of hope
alone and off path
no sight of the pack
no guide points home

the dark of night
has fallen
holding the light
a prisoner in dark recess

there is no reason
no direction to trust
no reason to know
emptiness as fair

yet existing in the dark
lighting our ways
when all help
avails not

it brings
something
something forgotten
some lift in the heart

ride the current
find a new course
leave emptiness behind
hold firm, don't look back

hope gives light
trust is strength
love brings meaning
leading a new way home

Your way

my as it should be is predictable
it's a cut path
well traveled
understood
clear lines

your as it should be
taking me away
from what i control
down fresh paths
made as we go

past beauty
past danger
but it is safer
because you're here

Wicked

i see my fear
i see my doubt
my flight to self
others abandoned

i see me as good
yet fly to self
when scared and alone
i am what my heart seeks

who knows our selfish depth
free me
free me
free me

love gives life purpose
to those who don't see, its foolishness
love for you will spring in my life
love for others will be my mark

Others and i

Judging Others

callous eyes
emptied hearts
judgments cast easily
faults found so clearly

briefly passing
feeling only distance
but an eye to critique
seeing only difference

left, lost in dust
no love for them
others condemned
no patience follows

how can we?
how dare we?
are we the better?
are we better than all?

Worthy?

they told me, i am not worthy
i deserved what had happened
not worthy of freedom from pain
my worth was measured by my pain
not worth, of what love had given

they were right
i am not worthy
they were wrong
you gave me worth
you set me free of this pain

how good is love
i get what i don't deserve
this worthiness i didn't earn
i am now, graciously valued
not by my actions but by love

inescapable, un-cover-up-able, damning!
my imperfections are inexcusable
you call me your child
you call me yours
i belong

Candle

i am a crushed candle
crumbled bits of wax
useless cotton wick

purpose extinguished
on the table exposed
shame laid bare
no ones way lit

gentle is love
seeing what was
knowing what can be
gently, not soft

moulding the wax
placing its wick true
gently holding it togeather
using heat as a glue

taking more wax
from a store on the shelf
love carefully restores
this candle's true self

Growth

i am stretched beyond all i knew
instead of breaking me
i am broken in
growth comes again

an ocean crossing vessel
reaching the other side
passing storms
driving hard to landfall

rest for body and mind
taste of sweet fruit
the joy of the land
loved ones flourishing

my heart is enriched
my posting is firm
blessed is my soul
stretching has ceased

More with love

something inside died
i am less but more i am
my center was full of just me
death made room for love

strong was my imperfect
short, needing height
love picked me up
met my weak with might

letting love in was a small death
releasing awakening relief
no longer just me in here
free to be more than i could have been

revealing to me truth
you guide me deeply
from deepest inside
i am more me, with you

Turn your way

looking back i see
hours, days wasted
in my time of need
did i bend my knee
did i turn to you

i went looking
looking to see me
my eyes saw only me
what i could've been
what a waste!

now i turn
i look to see
you're waiting
calling me

longing for
me near to you
my approach to you
to hold me close

but all i do
is keep the gap
that separates
me from you

locked in fears
i bound myself
love setting me free
from a cage of disconnect

from misery
from meanderings
to follow this path
you guide me on

mustering might
to get home tonight
through the doors
resting safe in life

let not my eyes be thrown
from ways of your own
allow me to serve
and know you

standing on your path
a light posted in place
illumination of the way
to eyes that can't see home

have i honour to ask this request
i have none
with what can i stand
and ask from such as one

by your bloody gift i know
i have access to your throne
by your mercy
i can seek you alone

help me know the power of grace
when you touch me with love
when you visit me
i am changed

he bound the atom
he can split a heart
i am open
be in me

Love's purpose

Live for Love

oh the pleasure
oh the pain
it comes from knowing
it's all the same

wake up one day
go around and do things
the same in every way
to every other day

study meaning
see purpose here
understand what you do
every time you put on shoes

you think you know
what to do in this life
you've got it cornered
with your hands tied

blow the lie
it's just a joke
your life
it ain't your own

live for love
serving love
love others
love love

Not buying

i don't buy your words
i don't buy your scene
what are you thinking
what do you mean

playing games
that will break your heart
messing with things
that tear you apart

only love can set you free
from this misery
only love is the way
from your mess today

you've been on your own
you've been alone
now its time to meet
he who can set you free

you've heard of him before
now let love in the door
open your life to him
love will set you free

don't ignore who beckons you near
the path you're on is rarely neat
finding the best way to spend
the days coming your way

i'm living glory out
it's a beautiful way to be
knowing i've been set free
living hope, trusting love

Love gives hope

I am led

my feet are led
my heart is called
my mind wanders this path
your journeys are new

you keep me safe
their walls of fear
threaten to overwhelm
you stand behind, beside and before me

they threaten my existence
seeking to destroy me
my safe companion
you are my safety

you need me not
though i need you
you call me to you
i only answer

sometimes responding
barely at all
yet you seek
yet you call

you hold me from destruction
you have been my friend
you have been my rock
you are my god

i could never repay
nor do you ask
you have loved
i have not

My heart kneels

beautiful lord
my heart loves you
your essence i worship
let my life show the same

coming before you
standing in your space
lifting hands in surrender
to my god, who calls me saved

heart yields before you
do with me what you will
but keep me your own
laying my life before your throne

frequently failing
perfection lived never
love has not left me alone
always calling me, loves own

calling me by name
understanding my pain
letting me see this care
not leaving my despair

when my heart cries, you hold me
lifting me when i feel like dying
when my world falls apart
love is sowing back parts

landing on my back
you gently let me rest
strength drained to go on
you quicken me again

filling my heart with joy
thankful words flow
in you finding
freedom

you're placing
hope in me
from you
i am learning love

Whisky

the makers mark
indelibly written
deep within my heart

calling of the raw
yearning and churning
wanting to be known

to know and feel
finding our part
of more than we are

More than life

lord be to me
more than the food i eat
my wife i lay beside
more than this life

your presence
my continued dwelling
as i place myself
before your fire

may my words
my acts, honour, be this
so all who see me
see love

Life is raging fire

heart poured out for me
blood of life's raging fire
again breathe in me
i yearn your essence
put your life in me

raging fire
purging mercy
blinding kindness
pushing all aside

opening my heart
to know you
to see you

let me be your fire
burn in me

till i am pure love

i am living glory out
it's a wonderful way to be
knowing i've been set free

Trust love

Tool for Love

standing there
crowding around
all i hear is juke box
in a shouting crowd

having fun?
who they kiding
who are they fooling
avoiding pain, staying unfilled
just playing games

past the veneer
peer through the mask
seeing them clearly
who they really are
inner child avoided

make the connection
sucking on lollies hollow
empty promises
leaving them
unfulfilled

try and see
what love sees
past the mask
into the pain
reach their need

Tool for Love

i am love's tool
a hammer when needed
let me be a sculpture, please
but, i am a tissue with frequency

love sends help
in such unique ways
i am opening my door
for love to use all my days

Man of mettle

making mettle of this man
compassion bent heart
for the lonely
sick, the poor

bringing my mind to bear
on this task i am for
letting my attitude
be willing to roar

i will stand in the gap
i will not be moved
i stand not alone
but with love
for sure

thank you for letting me be me

                    me be me
                my lord use me
         let me be your connection

      to see this light that you give
          bringing new meaning
            glowing with life
             new connection

               this fresh life
             lets me see more
           making me bigger

                  i see you
              i see your pain
          the pain will remain
         you love so profoundly

                healing me
            you take my pain
           loving through it
              giving life
            giving fullness
            giving meaning

thank you lord
thank you for
letting me
be me

it's not how much love gives you
it's how much of you
is given to love
to use

Love Is

Evil is not

                    evil cannot be destroyed
                         evil is a choice
                        away from peace
                        away from love

                        without freedom
                        away from love
                          against love
                        no choice for love

                    evil cannot be destroyed
                      it can end, unchosen
                      drowned in choices
                    overwhelmed by love

FAIRHEAD C.R.	HANRETTY R.H.
FARAGHER J.A.	HANTKE F.R.
FAULKNER W.G.	HARDMAN J.C.
FEALY F.J.	HARRISON J.H.
FELTHAM F.O.	HARVEY C.C.
FERGUSON E.J.	HAUGHEY C.S.
FERGUSON T.W.	HAWKINS E.S.
FERNYHOUGH S.	HEHIR A.
FERRY L.A.	HENRY G.J.
FISHER H.	HERBERT R.
FITZGERALD A.	HESKETH J.J.
FLANAGAN J.	HIGGINS S.
FLETCHER H.A.	HINE C.
FLORENCE J.W.	HITCHCOCK J.T.
FOLEY JAMES M.	HOBSON R.N.
FOLEY JOHN M.	HOCKING E.
FORSYTH T.G.	HODGKINSON O.
FOSTER R.A.	HODSON F.W.
FOY J.F.	HOGAN P.J.
FRASER C.C.	HOLMAN V.
FRASER H.J.	HOLST C.L.
FREARSON C.C.J.	HORNER E.W.
FREDERICK L.S.	HOWARD H.E.
FRUISH C.W.	HOWE I.J.
FRY T.L.	HOWITT N.W.
FULCHER C.H.	HUGHES C.E.
FULCHER J.	HUGHES G.H.
GARDINER N.B.	HUGHES J.P.
GARNOM J.	HUMPHRIES F.
GATLEY R.H.	HUMPHRY C.E.

No new thing

what song can i sing
that is unsung
what line can i say
as yet unsaid

what thought could be had
that's entirely new
in this universe
not one new thing

show me a new song
no song unrelated
no thought is alone
no word without peer

a word that came before thought
thought without intent
intent without space
space without love

bring me a tree
that had no seed
a man who just
came to be

show me a truth
not won with sweat
free my mind from
binding ties

the limits of the old
rebirth a new mind
love pours forth
my freedom

Just time

waves upon the shore
time immemorial
crashing crescendo
are we so sure

is this picosecond
adjacent to the next
or merged so slightly
it doesn't quite make sense

we can't be sure
if time runs backward
that all our behaviours
weren't thought of before

if time runs forwards
who can agree
if this restriction
applies just to you and me

do we die before we're born
do you know what that means
time traveling backwood
what would that be

do we follow a path
planned, predated
or just make a way
our choice of course

pre-programmed behaviour
lines of code
we find ourselves
short the equations

the riddle you see
the signs of times
path of your life
are they blurred

you may go forwards
much as you please
but what of love
the designer you see

...

before the world begun
actions were done
but little i see
until love came to me

timing constraints
binding you and me
holds not much weight
with one as is he

time limits love not
love's actions are free
to be there with you
to be here with me

Life changes

quickly
life changes
then slowly...
forever evolving

i did not know
five minutes ago
i would write this thing
who knows what tomorrow will bring

look around
open your eyes
drink in the sights
music and sound

limits unknown
potential to be more
a year ago you sang that song
now how does it go?

who can tell
what next year you'll know
follow love now
it's what will last

trust, hope and love
they merge in one

Love is my hope

I am not ashamed

          i am not ashamed
         love's gospel and name
            for it is this
       bringing me to this place

          my eyes have seen
          my ears have heard
             wonders done
             by your grace

          my heart has known
       nothing from love but love
            my life has never
             been untouched

             after so much
          given to lowly me
           how could i ever be
         ashamed of your name

Holy

holy is love
no one can touch that
love touches you

holy reaching out
extending over chasms
calling over waves of sin
and walls of distraction

grace stretching mercy
holiness gift to the trapped
undeserving masses
you and me

Hold tight

oh merciful
oh mighty love
hear my petition
here this night

save me tonight
powerlessly weak
threats overwhelming
spare me from this fate

grant me strength
to hold on to You
to hold tight

My hope is in you

my hope is in you
no woman or man can do

you hold me up
when my world tips

when my frailty scares me
when my legs fail me

when my life is shaken
when knives are drawn

when i tire of breath
i am but paper in the wind

my hope is in you

Keep me safe

keep me safe!
hide me from my enemies
who seek to harm me
forming weapons to destroy

when i step they hound me
shouting when i turn
lies hurled in my path
blocking my way

from their plans save me
let them not come to pass
rescue me from their grasp
when they grab and clasp

Religion is death

        peace by piece
      destructive sayings
    de-constructive idioms
   truth's intent enslaving
      meaning draining

       shells unfitting
      intent long lost
      world continues
     bereft of healing

      holding no hope
    of any intervening
     pain unendingly
   come hope & healing

can words express
this gratitude so deep
regardless of me, you love
i don't need to complete

you ask me to accept
this love so clean
i'd never known
love like this
but it's given to me

Worship

Deep ocean

                    weak feet
                    deep ocean
               running from pain
           to the call of freedom

                unleash my soul
               let my spirit soar
              i want to know you
            to live your freedom

I roll away

i roll away
i roll alone
on my knees
standing to face storms
threatening my home

bending my knees
i find a throne
i am safe and secure
because i know
his kind will endures

Rock & redeemer

rock, redeemer
lord, king
i kneel, i bow
i sing

you are king
you are worthy
i am your servant
let me go that far

my place
my hearts desire
,for you

i kneel
i serve
you are my king

Dad

my king , my dad
his love for me
beyond any other's

everything has he given me
against this i hold nothing
nothing to compare

i kneel to god
my king, my dad
receiving love

thank you
thank you
thank you

Throne

it's not my will or throne i make
his authority is uninhibited
given me while i obey
his grant is vast

unfailing love
unchanging one
in him is understanding
from him all meaning comes

his throne flows emboldening power
more than i can master
trusting in him
his will alone

he gives that which i do not own
reflecting his glory and under his throne
especially in situations i do not control
my trust is what he asks alone

surrendering to his throne
i trust in love alone
it is freeing to be
truly me

Melt

        the hardened of hearts
        melt before love
        this essence
        love

        love
        sparks praise
        my focus and ways
        surrendering all my days

Lord of lords

king over all kings
lord of the lords
supreme being
lord of me

yours, is
the kingdom of hope
bringing strength to me
meeting my needs

seed giver
breath of life
raiser of dead
near to me

life giver
raising my sight
sustaining this soul
making me whole

i am living glory out
it's a wonderful way to be
knowing i've been set free

I am love's

I am yours

it is calm
it is quiet
finding my pace

discovering my place
i am finding meaning
in surrendering to grace

your mercy is unfading
surrendering in your grace
i surrender to your embrace

i know no other grace
i know no other peace
your renewing mercy

wide is love's love
i have known no other
you are mine
i am yours

You are present

peace fills my soul
you are present

joy wells within
you are present

calmness settles on me
you are present

this love i know
has no other source

peace and love is here
as you are present

Refresh me whole

like spring water to my soul
you come, refresh
making me whole

pleasure of life
the joy of knowing you
fire spreads in my life

my skin prickles
emotions spark
my soul soars

grace's free gift
from my actions recourse
from condemnation i caused

knowing your freedom
peace calms my soul
free in peace

Sigh, Relax

breathe, relax....sigh
shivers run down my leg
let go, let it go
feel your eyelids close

the beer is nice
three wines, no wander
fear is all gone
feel peace

calm, no storm
it's been quiet of late
no harm, no mental mace
tending the garden has been easy

i have been walking in grace
thank you God
for all you've done
i'd be a loss without you

I will trust

i will trust
although i fear
i become dust
i will trust
though my way has filled
so much rust
i will trust
though it turns and grinds
and everything halts
i will trust
i drag myself
through the dust
i trust
i pull myself along
i yield
i fall
i lie there
i can't even crawl
i trust
i will hold whatever i can
yet i can't
so, i will trust.

i will let go
i will trust
i will yield
i will trust
i will relax
i will trust
i will lie here
i will trust
i will get up
i will trust
i will turn myself towards you
i will trust
i will put one foot in front of the other
i will trust
i will keep walking
i will trust
i will walk on
i will trust
i will get stronger
because i trust
because i trust
because i trust

I stand on the edge

my past has passed
standing on the jetty
at the edge of forever
this new journey ahead

sea mist rising
filling my lungs with hope
i know what was, was
what will come, will come

all that surrounds me fades
this world leaves for a moment
past recedes further
future lapping ever closer

i will be, what i will be
moving along my jetty
past left behind
i will be free

it's no longer my burden
love took it from me
paid for my missteps
love gives me new life

Stand in Love

                    the life of a man
                    in the eyes of god
                    how small a thing
                    how small our stand

                    we stand by his love
                    in grace from above
                    how small we must be
                could we be free if not for love

                    i have seen man
                    destroy many things
                    accidents or planned
                    things brake so easily

                    our strength
                    is nothing more
                    than his love
                    coming to us

Your will has joy

your will is kind
your will is good
your will is gentle
your will is fruitful

your will has joy
your will is peace
your will has pain
but it's pain that's employed

your will is to take me to meaning
to take me to the other side
your will is to take me there
away from where i have been

your will is hope
your will is peace
your will is release
your will is freedom

Surrender

your majesty
your grace
your pace
your will
i surrender

my way
detours
not safe
obfuscates
holding me back

a safe path
loves' gentle road
by refreshing water
leading gently uphill
your way is blessed

i follow your way
finding solace
in surrendering
to your embrace
find a peaceful way

As i am

                    my days
               be in your timing
                   your ways
               overtaking mine

               my heart dwells
                in your places
        my essence, permeated
              by your being

              my mind wander
          through your thoughts
          continually choosing
         to become, as you are

The laid path

love lays the path my feet walk
my eyes follow this leading light
bending my knee as i bow
saviour of all that has being

sealed on my heart and mind
dawn to dusk settles your name
love is the perfect, lifes first breath
precursor of existence, warmth of life's fire

passion of natures hidden desire
the yearning of life's rush
almighty
lord god

Yours is the way

i'd not wish my life on another
yet i'd not discard it either
love created me, calls me
shapes me to be

thank you for me
thank you for what others can be
thank you for setting me free
thank you for connecting me

your majesty
your grace
your pace
your will
i surrender

Saviour of mine

cushion of my life's blows
saviour of my heart and life
defender of my honour

my life is your's
my heart yields in your will
my feet step, to your purpose

you designed me this way
my heart, my bones
my eyes and nose

for this breath
for this life
thank you

www.ingramcontent.com/pod-product-compliance
Lightning Source LLC
Chambersburg PA
CBHW062111290426
44110CB00023B/2777